When we all get Together

by Heather Bradley

To Linda with a multitude of kisses.

When we all get
together
in the forest
of maple trees,

There will be a colony of
beavers,

A bevy of

otters,

A gaggle of
Canada geese,

A prickle of
porcupines,

A herd of

moose,

A nursery of
raccoons,

A sleuth of
black bears,

A clutter of
lynx,

A mischief of
mice,

A leash of
red foxes,

A scurry of

chipmunks,

A loveliness of
ladybugs,

A dray of
grey squirrels,

A sedge of
great blue herons,

A gang of
wolverines,

And a parcel of
white-tailed deer.

But when we see a scourge of
mosquitoes,

it is time to **leave!**

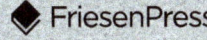

FriesenPress

One Printers Way
Altona, MB R0G 0B0
Canada

www.friesenpress.com

ISBN
978-1-03-911033-5 (Hardcover)
978-1-03-911032-8 (Paperback)
978-1-03-911034-2 (eBook)

1. JUVENILE NONFICTION, ANIMALS

Distributed to the trade by The Ingram Book Company

CPSIA information can be obtained
at www.ICGtesting.com
Printed in the USA
LVHW071606161122
733322LV00006B/244